John Richard Barlow

The City of Plague

And Other Poems

John Richard Barlow

The City of Plague
And Other Poems

ISBN/EAN: 9783744705509

Printed in Europe, USA, Canada, Australia, Japan

Cover: Foto ©Thomas Meinert / pixelio.de

More available books at **www.hansebooks.com**

THE

City of Plague,

AND

OTHER POEMS,

BY

JOHN R. BARLOW,

AUTHOR OF " JOHN'S TRIP, OR A VISIT TO NIAGARA,"
"THE THREE DEGREES," &C.

––––––

NIAGARA FALLS :

WILLIAM POOL, PRINTER,

GAZETTE BUILDING.

––––

1873.

^{TO}

L. C. BLIAL,

OF CHICAGO.

DEAR OLD TIME FRIEND :

My Boyhood's Pride!

Companion of youthful glee!
While memory dwells' mid scenes of yore,
My heart goes back to thee ;
And youthful hours, when innocence
Ruled every thought and word,
Come to my heart and make it beat,
As when in youth it stirred
In throbbing answer to the tones
Of Friendship, Love and Truth;
Oh, happy hours! oh, joyous scenes!
Oh, grand, immortal youth!
Year after year may come and go,
As wave on wave doth swell,
But memory like an undertow,
Brings back youth's scenes with brighter glow,
Those scenes we love so well,
The Sea of Life, like any sea
By storm is often tossed,

And many barks in sunshine launched,
    Are in the tempest lost;
But you and I have made our way
    Through weather fair and foul,
For though we've seen Dame Fortune smile,
    We've also seen her scowl;
She's played us many a doleful prank,
    Yet, still, we sail Life's sea;
You've reached a calm and sunny clime,
    While storms encircle me;
But Fortune's winds may make a shift,
    Or something turn the tide,
And you may be surprised some day
    To see me at your side;
Till then, accept this tribute, which
    An humble Poet pays,
To Thee, the chief of youthful friends,
To happy scenes of olden times
    And joys of other days!

JOHN R. BARLOW.

CONTENTS.

THE
CITY OF PLAGUE.

THE CITY OF PLAGUE.

———and all was black,
The brows of men, by their despairing light,
Wore an unearthly aspect, as by fits,
The flashes fell upon them. Some lay down,
And hid their eyes, and wept; and some did rest
Their chins upon their clenched hands, and smiled:
And others hurried to and fro, and fed
The funeral pile with fuel, and looked up,
With mad disquietude, on the dull sky,
The pall of a past world: and then again
With curses, cast them down upon the dust,
And gnashed their teeth, and howled.
                              —BYRON.

In a valley where the season
    Seemed forever summer time,
And the bright and golden distance
    Showed a gorgeous tropic clime,
Where a river downward rippling,
    With its murmur soft and low,
Filled the air with mellow music,
    While the zephers to and fro,
Wafted waves of sound melodeous,
    As the wavelets rose and fell,
O'er the silver corded beaches,
    Gemmed with pebble and with shell

Rose a city in that valley,
  Where from dawn till dewy eve,
From the rising to the setting,
  Did the sun his glory weave ;
Ne'er was fairer city builded
  Than that city of the vale,
Nestling to the grassy borders
  Where the river did assail,
Back unto the graded terrace
  Which the mountains overhung,
Where the echoes, once awakened,
  With a thousand voices rung.

Dwelt there in that city beauteous,
  Mortals of a haughty mien,
Proud of birth and grand possessions,
  Worldly wise and worldly vain ;
With the outer world no converse
  Would these haughty mortals hold,
Counted they themselves more worthy,
  Deigning not to be controlled ;
Deeming that themselves, self governed,
  Won such glory and renown,
As should sound through all the ages
  Through all time forever down.

And they built around their city,
　On the East, and North and West,
From the sun's bright place of rising,
　Westward, to his place of rest,
Only on the South their city
　Had no wall upbuilded high.
There the river onward gliding
　Gently flowed forever by ;
And its waters, pure, pellucid,
　Like some victor's burnished shield,
All the city in its brightness,
　As a mirror grand revealed.

And two gates of gorgeous splendor,
　Brazen built and grand of strength,
At the East and West they builded
　Thus to mark the city's length,
Then they gathered all in council
　And gave forth this one decree ;
That from other lands and rulers
　They should be forever free ;
Seeking succor from no nation,
　Giving help unto no land,
Keeping free and in their freedom
　They forevermore should stand.

On the hillsides sheep they pastured,
  In the valley grain they grew,
And their mills were ever driven
  By the river running through ;
Rich they grew, and growing richer
  They forgot their rightful God,
Counted every call to duty
  As a seeming tyrant's rod,
And they grew to be ungodly,
  Called Religion, "Idle tale :"
Till Charity, at last forgotton,
  Was unknown within the vale,

Yet, withal, they seemed to prosper
  More than other cities round,
For within their walls of splendor,
  Plenty, only, could be found ;
While a Famine came and wasted
  All the cities lying near,
Yet *their* granaries were bursting
  With the surplus of the year,
And they laughed to scorn the wretches
  Who without each mighty gate,
Cried for bread to ease their hunger,
  Begging piteous, ear' and late.

Night and morning, from the dawning
  To the waning of the light,
From the deep'ning of the shadows;
  Through the watches of the night,
Morn and even, noon and midnight,
  Round that city in the vale,   .
From a thousand starving mortals
  Came that ceaseless piteous wail :
"Give us bread!" "Oh from the fulness
  Which the Lord hath given you,
Grant a mite to fellow mortals
  Let us not thus vainly sue."

But within that gorgeous city,
  On the ear and to the eye,
All unnoticed stood the wretches,
  All unheeded fell their cry ;
As in light of lavish splendor
  Rolled the careless, heartless throng,
While the hand of Heaven, unmindful,
  Seemed to be withheld too long ;
And as louder and more mournful
  On each new succeeding morn
Grew the wail without the city,
  Deep and deeper grew their scorn.

And the gates were closed and guarded,
    While along the river side,
There their sentinels were posted,
    So that every one who tried
For an entrance to the city
    Might be caught and quick expelled,
Thus the throng of starving creatures
    In their misery were held
From the fortune favored mortals
    All aloof, while in their pride,
All the woes of those around them
    They did mock at and deride,

But a Prophet rose among them,
    One, a man of heart and age,
Who through all the streets lamented
    Near approaching heaven's rage:
" O ye dwellers in this city
    Fairer than ere erst was known,
Think ye not that cries and prayers
    Reacheth up to Heaven's throne ?
'And that multitude of wailers,
    Who without your city walls,
Cry for bread, and retribution,
    Shall in vain repeat their calls?"

"Thrust him out!" a thousand voices
　Cry in mingled rage and scorn,
"Let his wailings up to heaven,
　With the other wails be borne."
And without those gates of beauty,
　He was quickly seized and thrust,
And no friend advanced to save him,
　Nor was offered him a crust:
And he cried, while yet the hinges
　Creaked the closing of the gate,
"Curst above all cursed cities,
　Ye but hasten on your fate."

And without that guarded city,
　Cruel Hunger, gaunt and lean,
Traced his lines upon each feature,
　In each shrunken form was seen.
Friend from friend, would turn in anguish,
　Seeking each his pain to hide,
Till the darkness hid each feature,
　Then they sat down side by side.
Side by side, and hand hand clasping,
　Through the long, lone hours of night
Till the shadows woke and vanished,
　At the call of morning light.

But from 'mong each group of watchers,
    At the waking of one morn,
Sadder, deeper and more mournful,
    Were the wails of anguish borne.
All before their guest was hunger,
    Only hunger and no more,
But another now they numbered,
    Which they had not known before ;
Death had spread his poisoned pinions,
    And where friends at eve had lain,
Lay but corses, thin and shrunken,
    That should never wake again.

And the sound of lamentation
    Rose upon the morning air,
And their hunger seemed forgotten
    While beside their loved ones there,
Knelt the living, weeping, wailing,
    And the air, their cries did fill,
Till at ev'ning round the corses,
    Sat the living, sad and still.
For they knew not ere the morning,
    With Death's shadows overhead,
Who of them would leave the living,
    Who of them would watch the dead.

And, as morning light appearing
  Raised the vail of gloomy night,
Saw the watchers, other loved ones
  Had departed with the night;
Thus continuing, each morning
  Saw the mourners fewer grown,
While the valley with the mourned for
  Was each morn more thickly strewn,
And the air became more loathsome,
  More and more as days wore on,
For the corses all unburied
  Lay beneath the burning sun.

'Neath the sun they lay and blackened,
  And each mourner, hunger's slave,
Only mourned the more because he
  Had not strength to dig a grave ;
Thus they lay, no strength, no motion,
  Lying, dying, day by day,
While the corses still increasing
  'Neath the sun did more decay;
Till at length the air becoming
  Charged as with a mist of death,
All remaining soon were stricken,
  Breathing death with every breath.

Till a murmur ran among them
  Indistinct at first and vague,
Then a cry, wild, deep and mournful,
  "We are doomed it is the Plague!
Then arose the Prophet trembling,
  As his limbs beneath him fail,
And his bony finger pointing
  T'ward the City of the vale,
Thus he cried: "Oh, City scornful!
  God with you doth now engage;
Thou art doomed, and I, your victim,
  Shall be bearer of his rage!"

"Up!" he cried to those around him,
  "Up! I give you God's command,"
"Fear ye not your strength shall fail you
  When upheld by his strong hand;
Look upon yon gorgeous City,
  Bright above it are the skies;
Dwell therein the proud, hard hearted,
  Who have heeded not your cries;
But I tell and tell you truly,
  All their grandeur shall decline,
We are instruments of justice,
  Vengeance saith the Lord is mine!"

"See yon gate of strength upbuilded,
.Doubly guarded night and day;
See yon river grandly flowing,
   There their sentries guard the way;
See yon beetling cliffs o'erhanging
   On the north the city's rear;
Guarded thus, how proud their bearing,
   Thinking they have nought to fear;
But they heed not in their folly
   That a road doth open lie
To the heart of their fair city
   Where who meeteth us shall die,".

"Up yon steep and jagged mountain,
   Down from thence a winding path,
Once that road were traveled, all their
   Power cannot stay God's wrath;
In our veins the dreaded Plague tide
   Courses wilder every hour,
And when once we gain their city
   Futile all their boasted power;
For we carry death within us,
   Every breath exhaled shall bear
Death and mourning to each hearthstone,
   Plague and horror in the air.

Though Plague stricken, two arising,
  With the Prophet upward go ;
Though their breath comes faint and fainter,
  And their steps are weak and slow ;
Up the rugged mountain scaling,
  Upward, westward till they stand
Just above that fated city,
  In the sunlight bright and grand ;
And the waves of mellow sunshine
  Gild each casement with their glow,
Bathing in a golden glory
  All the guarded wealth below.

Spake then one of the Plague stricken :
  " On such beauty and such wealth,
On this city where they know not
  But of happiness and health.
Is it right that we should bring them,
  Unsuspecting every ill,
Death, disease and dire destruction,
  Every home with woe to fill ?
Think ye, were it not far better
  That this mission we forego ?
' Tis but death if here we linger ;
  ' Twill be death as well below."

"Oh! ye vacillating mortal,
    Oh! ye form with puerile heart,
Dost thou dare to chide Jehovah?
    In His vengeance to take part
Wouldst thou dare refuse?   What melting
    Of their hearts was there for thee?
Wherefore, thus their scorn forgiving,
    Shouldst thou from thy duty flee?
Onward! downward! death! destruction!
    Bearing as we pass along,
Thus repaying all their scorning,
    Thus returning all the wrong!"

Then adown that mountain pathway,
    Slowly with a trembling pace,
Through the streets of wealth and grandeur
    Till they gained the Market Place;
And as onward, never turning,
    They their weary way pursue,
Halt the 'habitants in wonder,
    Asking each if these they knew?
But to none of all that city
    Are the dying strangers known,
As they press to end their journey,
    While each step brings forth a groan.

"Ho, ye strangers to the city!
   Whence, and wherefore are ye come?"
"Do ye come from up the valley?"
   "Wherefore silent? Are ye dumb?
But the strangers never heeding,
   Still unanswering, wend their way;
To the right or left not turning,
   Heeding not what passers say;
"Hold!" cried one, "I know their leader,
   'Tis the Prophet who arose,
Dooming us to beggars' curses
   If we heeded not their woes."

"Are the gates not closely guarded?
   And the river side as well?
How then, could they gain the city
   Here their cries of woe to swell?"
"See! they reach the city's centre,
   There they halt and take their stand,
Fearful trio, thin and shrunken,
   Grasps each bloodless hand a hand,"
"Oh ye wand'rers lean and lanken
   Have ye come from 'mong the dead?"
"List! ye scorners, cease your scoffing,
   We are beggars come for bread!"

"What? beggars in our city?
　Beggars from the vale,
Where daily, without ceasing
　They tire us with their wail?"
"Was't o'er our walls so mighty,
　Or through our gates so strong,
Or by the river's border
　Ye made your way along?"
Neither walls nor gates nor river
　Our entrance here hath shared,
We entered here at God's command,
　The way by God prepared."

Then through the streets and by-ways
　These words all do proclaim,
"Lo! in our Mart stand beggars
　To mock us with their shame!"
And the rich and lordly masters
　Of the city, passing by,
Laugh in scorn and shun the wretches
　And taunt them while they cry
"Oh! Prophet; in your hunger,
　Where now your boasted power?
Where now the God you vaunted
　Could crush us in an hour?"

Thus they taunt with scorn and laughter,
    While the beggars on the pave,
Feel the stones their dying couches,
    The city's fate their grave ;
See the mighty of the city
    Unheeding pass them by, .
While within great plenty's circle
    They lay them down to die ;
See the daughter of a million
    Gather closer up her dress,
Lest the garment touch the pavement
    Which a beggar's foot doth press.

Thus the day at last is ended,
    The night wears on apace,
And morning finds them standing
    Still within the Market Place.
"What! ho! ye guards on duty!
    Who keep the city's gates,
Thrust forth these noisome beggars,
    Their fate without awaits ;
Behold those vultures circling
    O'er the valley far away,
Thrust out this making carrion
    And give the birds their prey !"

"Thrust out this making carrion?
  Yea, thrust it out who will ;
Those vultures o'er the valley
  Will wait yet longer still."
Thus spoke the Prophet, while the fire
  Of vengeance in his eye,
Filled those with dread who round him stood
  To see him sink and die.
And thus again he spoke to them:
  "Oh! mortals, cease to scorn,
A weight of woe is on you such
  As ne'er before was borne?"

"God blessed and gave this city
  A plenty over all,
Yet when he asked a tithing
  Ye heeded not his call;
Without your gates, his people
  Lie dying day by day,
What penitence of empty words,
  Can wipe this sin away?
But penitence ye have not known,
  Nor do ye know it yet;
The daily woe around you has
  Your hearts but harder set."

"Then hear the doom Jehovah sends:
  For all your taunts and scorn,
Your city of its glory shall
  Forever more be shorn;
I spoke to you the warning words,
  Ye heeded not my cry.
But with the ones for whom I plead
  'Ye thrust me out to die;
And now God sends the words of doom
  By him who warning gave,
This city was my cradle, and
  Her dust shall be my grave !"

"Your piles of monumental wealth,
  Your mansions old and new,
Whose burnished casements in the sun
  Beam brightly to the view,
The gates you set to guard your wealth,
  Your walls as grand and high,
Shall be your curse, for from the vale
  Through them you may not fly;
The gates by power than yours more great
  Are barred, not oped shall be;
The walls shall be as glass to those
  Who by their way would flee."

"The river, where your sentries' tread
  Is echoed night and day,
Shall be to you a boiling lake
  To bar your outward way;
The mountain wall which God hath set
  To guard your city's rear
Shall fill your hearts with deepest dread,
  And whelm your souls with fear ;
Those mighty crags by time unmoved
  Your fleeing steps assail,
And from yon frowning brow shall sweep
  A tide of molten hail,"

" Ye think my words are idle, all,
  And vain as empty air,
Then learn that every word is truth,
  God's vengeance I but share ;
Behold these wretches at my feet,
  Ye think they lie asleep,
Yea, so they do, but not on earth
  Shall end repose so deep ;
They sleep in death ; oh, endless sleep !
  No power death's tide can stem ;
Come gaze on death, and learn to die,
  Ye soon shall sleep with them."

"See how each feature hath been racked
  With throes of agony,
Come, look, for in your veins doth roll
  The curse which here you see;
See how they blacken in the sun,
  Behold the fever here,
Within my veins the doom-tide runs,
  Ye start? 'Tis late for fear!
"Then know." and here his voice sank low.
  " No more my words be vague;
My hour hath come, I leave with you,
  My curse, the Eastern Plague!"

Sank his voice down to a whisper,
  And his eyes grew glassy dim,
And, upon the pave down sinking,
  Death came welcome unto him;
Then throughout the throng around him
  Ran a thrill of mortal fear,
Face with dread on each face gazing,
  Saw the curse imprinted there;
Each from each in horror turning
  Seeks his home in haste to gain;
All too slow their quickened footsteps,
  Late their fear, their haste in vain.

As the course of streams in spring time
   Are increased by melting snow,
So the tide of life in fever
   Through the veins doth swifter flow;
As the streams already swollen,
   By new streams are further swelled,
So the blood already fevered
   By the Plague is more impelled;
Swift and wild, and wilder, swifter,
   More increasing every hour,
Till the heart at last consuming
   Sinks beneath the lava power.

Thus within that guarded city,
   Ran the life tide faster now,
While the fever gaining fullness
   Stamped its impress on each brow;
Doors were barred and casements bolted,
   Every street deserted, drear,
While the air seemed all down laden
   With a weight of deadly fear;
While within each habitation
   Echoed every wall the cry,
" 'Tis the hand of retribution,
   We are smitten, and we die!"

And when night with sable mantle
   Shrouds the city with her gloom,
Every household seems enfolded
   By a pall of rayless doom;
Every light burns dim and dismal,
   Struggling with the vaprous air,
Oh, for morning! oh, for sunlight!
   Every heart repeats the prayer;
Sunken eyes on loved ones gazing
   Meets but with a wilder stare,
Burning hands press fevered foreheads,
   Horror, horror every where!

Night dies! oh, death of dreary stillness!
   Morn wakes! oh, birth of darkness born!
Better for night's death eternal,
   Than the birth of such a morn;
Slowly, as if loath, the darkness
   From the coast of morning rolls,
But no sunbeams with their brightness
   Chase the phantoms from the souls;
Dull the sky, a leaden dullness,
   Copper tinted here and there,
As. at sea, a fire far distant,
   Horror, horror everywhere!

O'er the valley to the Eastward
    Rolls the mist of morn away;
O'er the valley to the Westward
    Wakes the morn to beauteous day;
On the mountain top appearing
    Sport the sunbeams bright and clear;
O'er the plain beyond the river
    Breaks the day without a tear;
Only o'er that fated city
    Are the shadows overthrown,
All around, the day is brightness,
    Horror, horror there alone !

Slowly downward from the mountain,
    Settling like a funeral pall,
Rolls a cloud of noisome vapor,
    Gathering dampness over all;
From the side of every mansion,
    From each stone in every wall,
As if born of silent weeping,
    Slow the vaprous tear drops fall;
And the air grows close and stifling,
    And each casement open thrown,
Lets the vaprous horror enter,
    Horror, horror there alone.

Now a wail of deepest anguish
  To each ear the dampness bears,
Death hath made his formal entry
  And the first his mantle wears;
Toll the bells! the first hath answered
  To the Prophet's dying curse;
Dig the grave! no time for mourning!
  Haste and call the burial hearse;
Toll again! another answers!
  Ere its echoes die away,
Still another, and another,
  Ceaseless tolling all the day.

Now once more the darkness falling
  Ends the day, but not its woes,
Sombre arch! Unbroken darkness!
  No respite and no repose.
Death holds now unhindered revel,
  Soft his footsteps tread the gloom;
While his fingers touch the foreheads
  And his victims feel their doom;
On the morrow, cease the tolling,
  'Tis a vain and useless task,
Death hath need of no revealing,
  He hath lain aside his mask.

'Tween the darkness of the midnight
   And the gloom of middle day,
Scarce they judge, for but a twilight
   Bears the awful arch away ;
But through every street and by way
   Falls the bearers' ominous tread,
While o'er all the mighty wailing
   Sounds the cry, " Bring forth your dead !"
Oh the depth of untold horror
   In that dread appalling sound,
Is there no escape, no succor ?
   Can there no release be found ?

Fire ! build fires throughout the city !
   Where'er street crosses street,
There let the bright red fire flame
   The Death Plague current meet !
Raise high the sparkling altars,
   Nor distance long between,
Till in a fire gilt border
   Returning life is seen ;
Till from our beauteous city
   The death cloud rolls away,
And from our night of horror
   Breaks forth a brighter day.

Then to light the flames they hasten,
  That the Fire Fiend,—who in wrath
Knows no master—should in triumph
  Sweep the Plague Fiend from their path;
And as up the flames ascending
  Bears the vaprous cloud away,
They shout deliverance and triumph
  From and o'er the Plague Fiend's sway ;
And still in their mad excitement
  Raise the altars higher still,
Till a mighty flame of triumph
  Doth the whole great city fill.

But their triumph turns to sorrow
  And their joy soon turns to woe,
For the power they call to save them
  Doth now no master know ;
And the bright flames sweeping higher
  Light the mansions dull and grey
And the Fire Fiend in his hunger,
  Claims the city as his prey,
And the 'habitants in anguish
  This new ruin doth foresee,
And from out their fire doomed city
  They quickly turn to flee.

To the gate they wildly hasten,
  But the bars are doubly sure,
They have melted in their sockets,
  Are immovably secure.
Then they bring their scaling ladders,
  O'er the walls to make their way,
But their efforts all are futile,
  For the Fire Fiend holdeth sway ;
O'er those walls of seamless cement
  He hath caused the flame to pass,
And where erst had stood their ladders
  Is a front of glist'ning glass.

Then they haste to gain the river,
  But from it they quick recoil;
For the flame hath lapped its border,
  And its waters seethe and boil ;
But one other way remaineth
  To escape the fervent tide,
Ere the red tongued tyrant grasp them,
  Up the steep set mountain side ;
But the flame sweeps on before them,
  Bearing terror to their souls,
For adown the heated mountain,
  Now the loosened lava rolls.

And the flame they seek to flee from,
   Licks the ground their feet doth tread,
And the fiend their hands did summon,
   Their bodies now hath fed ;
Still the flames swept ever onward,
   Surging all that night and day,
While beyond that city's borders
   Roll the burning clouds away ;
Till where hung the dark Plague shadow
   Like a pall the day before,
Hangs the sun a seeming blood spot,
   In a field of deeper gore.

And every form and substance
   Crumbled 'neath the fiery wave,
Till the dust of that fair city
   Was in truth the Prophet's grave,
For that city in its ashes
   Had forever gone to rest.
Ere the sun in gory brilliance
   Sank adown the bleeding west.
MORAL.—Tis a tale of which the moral
   Forever more should live :
If God unto *you* hath given,
   'Tis but meet that you should give.

OTHER POEMS.

THE LAND BEYOND THE TIDE.

I am thinking, sadly thinking
Of life's joyous happy morn ;
Ere my heart lay mangled, bleeding,
By its sorrows rudely torn ;
And my spirit sadly turning
To those happy days of yore,
Reads in anguish on their pages,
Joy on earth, ah, nevermore !
And the shadows falling darkly,
That sweet promise seems to hide,
Of a happy home immortal
In the land beyond the tide.

I am dreaming of the maiden
With her eyes so deeply blue,
Looking out a faithful index
Of the heart within so true,
Thinking of her heav'nly beauty,
And her wealth of tresses bright,

She a picture of an angel;
In a frame of living light;
And her form, as in a halo
Seeming evermore to glide,
Like an angel sent on mission
From the land beyond the tide.

I am thinking of the sunshine
Which like glory filled my heart,
And the happiness unbounded
Seeming of myself a part,
When the blessed, sweet assurance
Was by her unto me given,
Over power of death to triumph,
Mine on earth, and mine in heaven;
And my spirit backward turning
Sees us sitting side by side,
As we sat, and sang together,
Of the land beyond the tide.

Never thought I then of sorrow,
Never heart more light and free,
All was heav'n to me on earth then,
All on earth was heav'n to me;

She was mine, then, and mine only,
And I deemed her all my own,
Oh, sweet dream! how vain, delusive,
And the waking, oh how lone!
Cruel death my claim ignoring
Sought and claimed her as his bride,
And an angel came and bore her
To the land beyond the tide.

Then a darkness fell upon me,
All of love was lost to me;
And I sank me deeper, deeper,
In a sea of agony;
And my soul surcharged with sorrow
Strove the dreamlike bands to break,
But alas! the dream was real,
And from it I ne'er shall wake
Till I reach my home immortal
On the far off thither side,
And a spirit claim my angel
In the land beyond the tide,

But, between my spirit's haven

And its present chafing cell,
Runs forever down a river
With a mighty roll and swell,
And my spirit gazing wistful,
Up from out its prison bars,
Sees the home it longs to enter
Just beyond the twinkling stars;
And, beyond that mighty river
Rolling down so dark and wide,
Faintly shines the terraced glory
Of the land beyond the tide.

And, beyond the distant outline
Of that holy mystic shore,
Rises up the jeweled city
Which shall stand forevermore!
And the walls of purest jasper,
Shining 'neath a setless sun,
Tell in glowing words immortal
Of a glory just begun;
And, my spirit wild, rebellious,
Scarce its destined time can bide,
Longing so to see the glory
Of the land beyond the tide.

But, I feel that soon the angel
Will return to set me free,
And I'll journey o'er that river
To the home prepared for me;
Though the waves forever surging
Sweep tumultuous o'er my soul,
They shall not prevail against me
As they madly seethe and roll;
For I know that when I'm sinking.
I shall see my spirit's bride,
Reaching down her hand to guide me
To the land beyond the tide.

DEATH OF THE OLD YEAR AND BIRTH OF THE NEW.

Mourn! mourn! a friend is dead:
　　The Old Year is no more;
Last night his weary spirit fled
　　Beyond Time's mystic shore.

We mind the hour when he was born,
　　A laughing, joyous child;
He burst upon us at his birth,
　　With spirits light and wild.

We watched his tender, tottering steps
　　Adown the glade of time,
Till birds in leafy, springtime bowers,
　　Their notes of praise did chime.

We watched his firmer youthful steps
　　Still strong and stronger grow;
Until we saw his manhood's crown
　　'Neath sun of summer glow.

We watched his onward conquering march,
  As time by him was slain;
But woke, too soon, alas! to note
  His manhood on the wane.

He watched him tottering on the verge;
  Then saw him downward turn
To lay beside his kindred dead
  His ashes in the urn.

We watched him down the silv'ry tide;
  His course was nearly run;
His lab'ring breath came faint and low,
  His weary task was done.

We watched beside his dying bed
  As sombre death came down;
We closed his eyes and turned away
  To feel a friend had gone.

There, in the tomb of ages dead,
  He slept this Sabbath morn!
Yet, from his ashes, Phœnix like,
  The glad New Year was born!

He comes to us with smiling face,
  With mirth and laughter gay;
Then let us hearty welcome give
  On this his natal day.

The Old Year is dead! we mourn!
  We drop the kindred tear;
Yet, shall we mourn him still, and weep,
  And linger at his bier?

Old friends must die! yet new ones come
  E'en ere we say farewell;
The same bells chime the New Year's birth,
  That toll the Old Year's knell.

Then cast all dreary thoughts aside,
  Begin with life anew;
What if our life a dark side has?
  It has a bright one too!

Then hand in hand, we'll forward press,
  All care we'll throw away,
And cheerful start with life anew
  This joyous New New Year's Day!
JANUARY 1st, 1871.

WILL YOU MEET ME UP IN HEAVEN, MOTHER DEAR?

Come and sit beside me mother,
Let me hold your hand in mine,
Move your chair a little nearer,
So the setting sun may shine
On the hand which I am holding,
As it falls in through the door,
For within the golden sunshine¡
I shall never see you more;
And I want to ask you, mother;
For I'm going far from here,
Tell me truly will you meet me
Up in heaven mother dear ?
Will you meet me up in heav'n, mother dear ?
       Mother dear !
Will you meet me up in heav'n, mother dear ?
  Where the angels are singing,
  And the sweet notes are ringing,
Will you meet me up in heav'n, mother dear ?

Raise me up a little higher
For the sun is setting fast,

And I want to see this sunset,
For I know it is the last
We shall ever see together,
For those clouds within the west,
Reaching far to north and eastward
In their golden glory dressed,
Hide the pearly gates of heaven
Where the angels all have met,
That are coming down to meet me
When the golden sun has set;
As they'll come to you from heaven,
  Mother dear! Mother dear!
If you'll meet me up in heav'n, mother dear?
  Where the angels are singing,
  And the sweet notes are ringing,
Will you meet me up in heav'n, mother dear?

See! the gates are moving inward,
Now they're standing open wide;
I can see the crystal river
And the land the other side;
And away beyond the hillside
Far beyond the other shore,
In a blaze of shining glory
Trembles heaven's inner door;

Do not hold me, dearest mother,
Do not fear that I shall fall,
For the angels now are with me,
And I hear my Savior call;
And I'm going up to heaven, mother dear!
　　Mother dear!
There to wait for you in heaven, Mother dear!
　Where the angels are singing,
　And the sweet notes are ringing,
Come and meet me up in heaven, mother dear!

OH WHERE HAVE THE ROSES ALL GONE?

I passed by the cottage to-day, Jennie,
  So cherished in mem'ries of you,
And gazed on the vine covered porch, Jennie,
  Where each side the sweet roses grew;
But the roses are faded and gone, Jennie,
  The cottage deserted and lone,
Oh! why has it changed so since then, Jennie?
  Oh! where have the roses all gone?

In the days fondly cherised by me, Jennie,
  Your cheeks with the roses were red,
From the sparkle which dwelt in your eye,
    Jennie,
  All sorrow and sadness had fled;
But scarce knowing I passed you to-day Jennie,
  Your cheeks were so pale, and so wan,
Oh! why have they changed so since then,
    Jennie?
  Oh! where have the roses all gone?

A wand'rer I've been since the eve, Jennie,
  We said our farewell at the gate,

But often my heart has gone back, Jennie;
　To mourn o'er your sad, sad too late!
But my wand'rings are over at last, Jennie;
　I'm returning heartbroken and lone,
And, I sorrow to think I have come, Jennie;
　To find that the roses are gone.

In reverie often I sit, Jennie,
　While memory, faithful and true
Bears me back to the days which are gone
　　　　Jennie,
　When thus I sat dreaming with you;
When with roses the pathway of life, Jennie,
　By fortune was lavishly strewn,
And I only awake from those dreams, Jennie,
　To find that the roses are gone.

Have the roses ot life proved to you, Jennie,
　As likely to fade and decay?
Has the view of the future you drew, Jennie,
　Proved shadow and faded away?
My heart goes back to that time, Jennie,
　Through the years that swiftly have flown;
And, I cry when I think ot those days, Jennie,
　Oh! where have the roses all gone?

THE NEW LOVE.

I have loved and been forsaken,
I have felt my heart awaken,
Waken, from its dream of fancied love and bliss;
    Now, a love my life is filling,
    All my soul with rapture thrilling,
For my former love was nothing unto this.

She I love, is free from guile,
And her artless, winning smile
Fills me with a love, to me before unknown;
    And I often sit and ponder
    On my life, and sadly wonder,
Shall I ever call this darling one my own?

Though I know she's not a fairy,
Softly tripping, light and airy,
Like Camilla, lightly skimming o'er the sea,
    Though I know she's not a JUNO,
    Nor a HEBE, yet, I do know,
She's the fairest of earth's daughters unto me.

Though the Nightingale when singing,
Fills the morn with sweet notes ringing,
Sounding through the summer air so lightly clear;
  Yet his song so sweetly trilled,
  Cannot move my heart once filled
With a melody to me more sweet and dear.

In her eyes, the love-light beaming,
Fills me with a nameless dreaming
Of the future, and what it may bring to me;
  And a hope is through me thrilling,
  All my soul with rapture filling,
But yet, something whispers, it can never be!

Oh! my love should not be hoarded,
Could there be to me accorded
Such a boon as mortal never won before.
  Though this hope I fondly cherish,
  Yet, I fear that it will perish,
And, I think of being friends, and nothing more.

And my soul in anguish crying,
Sees its airy castles lying,
Dashed in ruins, by a single, mighty "NO!"

And the rays of sunlight cheering,
In life's sky and disappearing,
As their place is filled by clouds of life-long woe.

Oft, I find the tears are falling;
At the thought, so dear, appalling,
And I feel already wrecked upon life's shore;
As the waves which now uphold me,
Seem upreaching to enfold me,
With the words forever sounding—Love no more!

Yet, take courage heart, I pray;
Ever darkest, 'tis, ere day;
Morning light may break athwart life's sky again!
And, my soul may feel the glory
Of that oft repeated story,
Loving and beloved:—In truth, and not in vain.

THE CLOSING OF THE DAY.

Twilight shadows gather round me,
   'Tis the evening of the day,
And the thoughts of care which bound me,
   With the sunlight pass away;
And the holy hour of evening,
   Round me casts it's witching spell,
As the zephyrs, perfume laden,
   Steal apast me through the dell,

As I watch the twilight fading,
   Watch the stars as they appear,
Thus, me thinks, my life is waning,
   And life's evening drawing near;
And the holy calm of twilight
   Foldeth o'er life's setting sun,
And I murmur not at knowing
   Life's sad, weary day is done,

DOWN THE AISLES OF TIME.

Down the Aisles of Time with wistful eye
   We gaze on the scenes of the past,
And memory glides 'mid the spectral forms
   Of shadow behind us cast;
And we sorrow to find so much of life
   Lying wasted along the way,
Made up of the moments heedlessly lost
   On our journey, day by day.

Down the Aisles of Time, where our weary feet
   Leave their prints on the wayside sand,
We are pressing on in the March of Life
   For none may idle stand;
Each moment of time is a precious gem
   We should guard whatever the cost:
Let us watch the jewels so when life shall end
   We can say that none are lost.

Down the Aisles of Time outstretching afar
   To the future, dark, unknown,

We strive, with our eyes, to pierce the vail,
   Which God in mercy has thrown
O'er the trials we'll meet, alas! full soon,
   For to each is lotted a share,
Yet be not dismayed for there cometh to none
   Aught more than his strength to bear.

Down the Aisles of Time still our footsteps tend
   As life's mystery we explore,
And ere long we shall reach that farther end,
   Leading out to the golden shore;
And soon, the dark vail will be lifted up
   So the light of our home we may see,
And soon, we shall pass from the Aisles of Time
   To a grand eternity.

WHY THE BABY DIED.

Why did the baby die? weep not fond mother!
E'en though thy treasure be gone from thee;
Thou knowest not from what pain and sorrow
Thy babe, an angel now, is free.
But thou did'st love her so? Ah, yes, fond heart!
E'en with a mother's purest, truest love,
But though thy love was great, a greater still
Dwells with the Lord of Heaven above.
Thy babe was very fair, and sweet, and mild,
God wanted her to dwell with him,
To sing hosannas with the angel throng,
And swell the ranks of cherubim.
Look round about thee through the earth, and see
What makes each home so gladly bright,
Is it not the babes, who fondly twine around
Each heart, filling them with happy light?
God took thy babe to wear an angel crown,
To make his home more bright and fair;
God sends the babes to gladden earth,
Yet, earth, her babes with heaven must share;
For what kind of heaven would heaven be,
If there were no *little* angels there?

BREAKING THE ENGAGEMENT.

Dear love ! 'tis just a year, to-day,
　You'll mind, since first I met you,
That meeting made me for all time
　All powerless to forget you;
And, as we grew acquainted more,
　More binding seemed your graces,
And deep within my heart I found
　Your image leaving traces.

You mind that eve I told my love,
　I drew you to me nearer,
You pressed your lips to mine and said
　None to you could be dearer;
That was a happy hour indeed,
　All earth to me was heaven,
Oh, precious troth ! from soul to soul,
　By lips, in kisses, given.

The days on wings of love flew by,
　Long happiness unbroken,

The bridal day was named by thee,
   Oh, joy to me when spoken !
The day has come; this is the morn;
   Alas a day of mourning,
For oh ! you ask me for release,
   Thy freedom thus returning.

Oh, surely, love, you cannot know
   The task you are imposing,
This is the end of all my joy,
   My future, dark, disclosing;
But if you'd have me let you go,
   Why I of course must let you;
And if you wish me to forget,
   Why hang you, I'll forget you!

THE DAWN OF THE NEW LIFE.

I have waited in the shadow
   While my life tide ebbed away,
Gazing through the shrouding darkness
   For the dawning of the day;
Long and dark hath been the night time,
   Long and dark, aye, dark and dreary;
Ever watching for the dawning,
   Sad and lone, and, oh! so weary!

But the night at last is ended.
   And the vigil now is o'er,
For the light of life eternal
   Lifts the darkness evermore;
And the angel of the Morning
   Back the mystic vail is holding,
And my weary eyes grow brighter
   As the *new life* is unfolding.

FROST PICTURES.

There are pictures on the window
　　Traced in crystal veins;
Light frosted on the window,
　　Frosted on the panes;
And as I gaze upon them,
　　Strange forms by me are seen,
As if some Fairy spun them
　　With waft of silver sheen.

I see the home of childhood,
　　I feel the joys I knew,
I wander in the wildwood
　　Where scented wild flowers grew;
And through my heart is thrilling
　　A gentle, mystic spell,
My soul with rapture filling
　　Beyond my pow'r to tell.

I wander in the old lot
　　Among the new mown hay,

I gaze into those blue eyes
   Where lovelight used to play;
I feel again the sorrow
   I felt when forced to part,
Alas! the long to-morrow
   That fell upon my heart.

And tears are coursing down my cheek
   For joys that's lost to me,
Joys of which I dare not speak,
   And joys I only see
In pictures on the window,
   Traced in crystal veins,
Light frosted on the window,
   Frosted on the panes.

SUNBEAMS.

Oft the clouds full dark and drear,
  Shroud the summer day;
Falling like a sombre pall,
  Drives the light away;
But the sunshine comes again
  With it's smile of cheer,
And the little sunbeams dance
  Earthward light and clear.

So it is all through our life,
  Sorrow's clouds come down,
Shrouding from our hearts the light,
  Bringing many a frown;
But, the clouds must sometime break,
  Then perchance will stray,
Brighter for the storm that's past,
  Sunbeams o'er life's way.

"IT IS NEVER TOO LATE TO MEND."

There's a maxim quite old, but yet it is good,
    And one you should keep in your mind;
It will ease you of many a troublesome thought,
    If you but obey it, you'll find;
This maxim though old will ever be new,
    And still to the right it will tend;
I give it to you as I found it myself,
    "It is never too late to mend!"

Ye Bachelors grim whom folly hath led
    To a *singular* waste of your life,
It'll just suit your case I'm sure you'll allow,
    And may help you in getting a wife;
What matter though you have been jilted in youth
    That's a dart Cupid often will send;
So while you bewail, keep this maxim in mind,
    "It is never too late to mend!"

Ye angular Maids of forty or so
    Pray don't give the battle up yet,

There ne'er was a stocking but mated a shoe,
   And doubtless, a husband you'll get;
For beauty is made, and age you can hide,
   And sense to your smiles you can lend;
With a scrub, rub and dub, keep this maxim in
      mind,
   "It is never too late to mend!"

Ye wretches whose hearts are as hard as the flint
   And crusted all over with sin,
Here's a chance to redeem, don't cast it aside
   But to mend all your ways pray begin;
There's a chance you'll allow that death may step in
   And bring all your schemes to an end,
So haste to reform with this maxim in mind,
   "It is never too late to mend!"

But, not to go over the whole human race
   And string out a mile of advice,
I'll speak to you all both aged and young
   And give you my mind in a trice;
(If you will but listen a moment to me
   And to take my advice condescend,)
And this shall be it, pray keep it in mind,
   "It is never too late to mend!"

ONLY A LITTLE BRAID.

Only a little braid!
Not a golden tress
With sunlight beaming o'er
To claim a wild caress;
Not a siken curl
Gracefully falling down,
Only a little braid,
Plain, and dark, and brown.

Only a little braid!
Yet, oh, how dear to me!
And oh, what scenes of joy
It brings to memory!
Not all the jeweled wealth
Within a kingly crown
Could buy my little braid,
Plain, and dark, and brown.

A LOVER'S GREATEST DISAPPOINT-
MENT.

When ADAM first in Eden
　　Began to live in bliss,
His happiness was incomplete
　　Until he got a Miss;
But when fair EVE was given
　　His happiness was full,
Yet, o'er his loving, simple eyes
　　She soon did draw the wool.

How pleasant must have passed
　　The golden hours, when they
Among fair Eden's bowers
　　Had nought to do but stray;
And when at eve they wandered forth
　　How happy was their fate,
With no old folks to grumble
　　If they came in too late.

No doubt, poor, simple ADAM
　　Was happy as could be,

I know just how he must have felt,
  It once was so with me;
But ah! poor, trusting lover,
  Though centuries have flown,
My heart goes back in pity, for
  His case was just my own.

He went on eve to see her,
  I'm sure 'twas Sunday eve,
And asked her out to take a walk,
  Alas! for him I grieve;
For, while he sat beside her
  Engaged in loving talk,
Old Nick himself came smiling up
  And took her out to walk.

With what a jealous anger
  His bosom must have filled,
When, to use a homely saying.
  He found his milk was spilled;
How heavy must have been his heart
  As homeward he did go,
Oh! ADAM I can pity you,
  For I have felt just so!

And ever since that evening,
  A Sunday eve I'm sure;
The deepest woe, the sharpest pang
  That mortal can endure,
Is when he's sitting by his love,
  Engaged in loving talk,
To have some other fellow come
  And take her out to walk.

A NOVEMBER STORM.

Hear how the wild tempest wails,
    And fierce assails
The firm-set walls, and loudly calls,
   As if to alarm
     Us, safe from harm.

How it madly rushes past,
    Blast, after blast;
With sigh and moan, and shriek and groan,
    How the sorrow swells
     It never tells.

Creep close to the sparkling fire,
    That leaps up higher
With wild delight this dismal night,
    As if 'twould engage
     The Storm King's rage.

Now let the fierce tempest whirl!
   And madly hurl
Its blinding darts at weaker parts,
   We're housed safely here,
    We have no fear.

Wail out your sad sorrow winds,
   That seeks, but finds
No place of rest, no haven blest
   Where you may alight
    This dreary night!

Pour now on each rattling pane,
   Oh ceaseless rain;
While storm imps leap, and revel keep,
   On each shrinking sash
    Your torrents dash!

Hark!—was that human cry?
   A moan, or sigh,
Borne on the air in wild despair
   From some sinking form
    Out in the storm?

Hush!—it may come again,
        Let silence reign!
No!—not again, the thought was vain,
          'Twas the tempest's shriek,
           Or fancy's freak.

List! the rain has ceased to pour;
        The winds no more
Their revels hold, but lie controlled
          By the Master's will,
           That "Peace, be still."

LIFE'S HILL.

To the hill ! to the hill !
To the hill together !
Hearts all joyous, light and free
In life's Spring-time weather ;
Fiery Youth with footsteps light,
To the hillside tending,
Eager to be on the way,
Eager for ascending.

Up the hill ! up the hill !
Up the hill ! together!
Manhood, every care surmounts
In life's Summer weather;
Faith sublime, and steadfast will,
In bright rapture blending,
Hand in hand, and heart to heart,
Each other firm defending.

Down the hill ! down the hill !
Down the hill together !

Hand in hand to reach the foot,
In life's Autumn weather;
Weary of the toil and care,
'Neath the years now bending,
Dreaming dreams of happy youth,
On the way descending.

From the hill! from the hill!
From the hill together!
Faded now youth's visions bright,
In life's Winter weather;
Feeble Age with step infirm
From the hillside tending,
Seeking only in the vale,
Rest when life is ending.

YOU'LL EVER BE YOUNG TO ME!

You have asked if I'll ever be true,
   If my heart will never change,
If I'll ever be leal to you
   As through the world we range;
You say that age will furrow thy brow,
   That your step will feeble grow,
But to me you'll be just the same as now,
   No change in thee I'll know,
   For you'll ever be young to me, darling,
   You'll ever be young to me;
Though age may furrow thy brow,
   And thy step may feeble grow,
   No change in thee I'll know
But ever the same as now,
   For you'll ever be young to me, darling,
   You'll ever be young to me.

You fear that I will inconstant prove,
   That my words are false and vain,
That in after years you'll lose my love,

That my heart you'll not retain;
But though age may turn to silv'ry white
 Rippling waves of beauteous gold,
And your eyes may lose their lustre bright
 And friends may call you old,
  Still you'll ever be young to me, darling,
 You'll ever be young to me;
Though age may furrow thy brow,
 And change the rippling gold,
 To me you'll not grow old
But ever the same as now,
 For you'll ever be young to me, darling,
 You'll ever be young to me.

And as we journey along through life
 Mid the thoughts of "Auld lang Syne,"
We'll lover like clasp our hands my wife,
 On the verge of life's decline;
Then shed no tears for the future years,
 You'll ever be young to me,
And be not troubled by idle fears,
 I'll ever be true to thee,
  For you'll ever be young to me, darling,

You'll ever be young to me;
Though age may furrow thy brow,
And thy step may feeble grow,
No change in thee I'll know
But ever the same as now,
For you'll ever be young to me, darling,
You'll ever be young to me.

DEARER TO ME.

Oh ! the sailor may tell of the wealth to be found
  In the depths of the ocean vast,
Of the coral and pearl that shine on the shore
  When the storm and tempest are past;
But the sparkling gems that tremble in light,
  May lie in their native sea,
For a glance from the eyes of the one I love
  Is dearer by far to me !

Oh ! the sages may tell of the wealth to be found
  In the pages of ancient lore,
Of the glorious feast of prose and of rhyme
  As they con their volumes o'er;
But the wealth that lies hid in the old time script,
  No matter how rich it may be,
Cannot equal one word from the lips I love,
  That's dearer by far to me !

Oh ! the miser may count o'er his hoarded gains,
  And gloat o'er his golden store,

And gather his wealth with a trembling hand
    From every clime and shore;
But the golden gleam that hardens his heart,
    He is welcome to keep, and free;
For a beaming smile, from the one I love,
    Is dearer by far to me!

Oh! Princes may tell of their gorgeous courts,
    Of their palaces, grand and high,
Of their gardens and parks, outstretching afar,
    So pleasing to royal eye;
But their palaces grand, their fields and parks,
    I care not to have, nor see;
For a simple cot with the one I love,
    Is dearer by far to me!

LAMENT OF THE SAILOR'S BRIDE.

On this lone sea shore,
Where the wild waves roar,
And dash up their beaten spray,
Here I sit forlorn,
From the early morn
Till the close of each weary day;
Here I wait and weep,
And my lone watch keep,
While the waves in their bounding glee
Chant a wild refrain,
As I watch in vain
For a form that is lost to me.

For beyond the wave,
In his island grave,
Where the wild flowers a bower have made;
There he sleeps alone
In the grave unknown,
Where his messmates their comrade laid;

And recks not that I
Ever sit and sigh,
Looking out from this lone sea shore,
Keeping watch in vain
O'er the mighty main,
For a form that will come no more.

O'ER BEYOND THE SHINING RIVER.

O'er beyond the Shining River,
There the angels sweetly sing;
And the souls immortal quiver
With the melodies that ring;
  Ever singing,
  Gently ringing,
Angels chant their sweetest lays,
Of a Lord and Saviour risen,
Ceaseless songs of endless praise.

O'er the river, safely anchored
On that bright and golden shore,
There the good and blessed are singing
Praise to God forevermore;
  Weary mortals
  Through the portals
Press to join the joyful throng,
As the friends who went before them
Gladly beckon them along.

See the countless number swelling,
Coming from the world below;
See the beams of heavenly sunlight
Make the waters brighter glow ;
  There gloomy fears
  And sorrow's tears
Shall ne'er again be known,
Nought but joy and gladness ever
Shall be felt in that bright home.

Surely death is not so dreary,
If the hope we only cherish
That the toil worn souls so weary
Though in death can never perish;
  But shall gain
  For every pain
A glorious recompense, far more
Than enough to pay the toiling
When they reach that Golden Shore.

YES, OR NO?

Dearest love! if when the sun
His diurnal course had run,
And the evening had begun
    After summer's sunny glow;
When through all the golden west,
Fleecy clouds in amber dressed,
Soft proclaimed the hour of rest
    To the night advancing slow;
Should I in the witching gloam,
From thy woodland cottage home,
Ask thee lovingly to roam,
    Wouldst thou answer yes, or no?

Did you thus consent to stray
In the pleasant twilight grey,
At the closing of the day,
    With the moon uprising slow;
And, if by thy prescence blessed,
Wild, entrancingly I pressed
To my heart, and fond caressed
    Thy sweet form, my love to show;

If upon a time like this,
In an ecstacy of bliss,
I should ask thee for a kiss,
    Wouldst thou answer yes, or no?

Still, if lovingly we strayed
In the pleasant sylvan shade,
Where the boughs dependent swayed,
    Gently sighing, soft and low;
Or if in the silv'ry beam,
In a wild, ecstatic dream,
All the world to me did seem
    Centered in thy weal or woe;
When my arm did round thee twine,
With my hand enclasping thine,
Should I ask thee to be mine.
    Wouldst thou answer yes, or no?

LOVE—SCORN—DESPAIR.

LOVE—

  Evening star appearing
  As thou seemest nearing,
  Hast thou aught endearing?
    Hast thou aught for me?
  Gentle zephyr winging,
  Love tuned anthems singing
  Tell me, art thou bringing
    Aught that's dear to me?
  River, ne'er returning,
  With thy voice of mourning,
  Tell me, art thou scorning
    While I ask of thee?
  Ever onward flowing,
  Whence and where no knowing,
  Hast thou heart for showing
    Pity unto me?

SCORN—

  At the morning's waking,
  When the day was breaking

Came no maiden making
    Thee her page to me ?
When the sun was soaring,
Hour of noontide scoring,
Sent she nought restoring,
    To my soul by thee ?
When the day was waning,
And the night was gaining,
Was no word sustaining
    Sent from her to me?
Was no token given ?
Have I vainly striven ?
Must my soul be driven
    On in agony ?

DESPAIR—
  Ah ! thy mournful moaning
  Is all hope dethroning,
  As the deep detoning
    Onward rolls from me ;
  She hath sent but scorning
  To my words love burning,
  River, ne'er returning,
    Bear me on with thee !
  Heart, thy wormwood drinking,

Why this coward shrinking
From the slight unlinking ?
    What is life to me ?
From her bitter scorning,
With my useless mourning,
River. ne'er returning,
    Thus I go—with thee !

ON THE RIVER.

On a river where the sunshine
'Mong the silver ripples played,
And the flower scented zephyrs
Fitful, wild and witching played,
By the breezes gently wafted,
Sailed a comely youth and maid:
　　Spake no word, but sailing there,
　　Built their castles in the air.

He, the lover, manly, noble,
She, his idol, sweetly fair;
They, both listless, idle dreamers;
But no threads of wordly care
Wove they with the golden texture
Of their castles in the air,
　　As they sailed that summer day,
　　Only youthful dreamers they.

But the lover gazing fondly
On the maiden by his side

Whispers words of love endearing,
As they gently, onward glide;
Pouring out heart's fondest treasures,
Seeking nought from her to hide.
 Love light o'er his features stealing,
 All his wealth of love revealing.,

Thus he spoke, his love outpouring,
"On the river of our life,
In the sunshine, in the shadow,
In life's elemental strife,
Whether joyous all our journey,
Or with storm clouds it be rife,
 All thy gladness let me share,
 All thy sorrows let me bear."

"Ere I answer," said the maiden,
"One small favor I implore,
As we're drifting idly onward,
Scarcely moving from the shore;
This I ask: your patience craving,
Teach me how to pull an oar!
 Nothing losing, I may gain,
 Though the wish may seem but vain."

To this wish so strangely seeming
He sought not to answer nay,
But the oar still holding firmly,
Tought her how, and showed the way,
Rowing onward down the river
On that sunlit summer day;
    Till at even's golden glow,
    She herself the boat might row.

Then, the maiden smiling sweetly,
Thus her answer to him gave:
"On the river of our life, love,
Fortune kissing every wave,
Trust and teach me in the sunshine
How to act when storms shall rave;
    Then, when wild winds beat the shore,
    I, perchance, may pull an oar!"

THE MUSIC OF THE HEART.

In each heart there ever vibrates
  To each voice a tuneful chord,
And there sounds the sweetest music,
  Trilled by ever loving word;
Like the harp, each separate chordlet
  Has its own peculiar range,
And each word, as it is graded,
  Makes the music's tuneful change.

Sometimes there arise discords, ·
  When the chords of love are crossed
By a voice that's toned in anger,
  And love's melody is lost,
As the heart strings, dumb and tuneless,
  Vibrate voiceless to and fro,
And the cadence dies to silence
  While the tear's notes noiseless flow.

But the sweetest, purest music
  Which the heart chords ever sound,

And in which all other love notes
    Die away in sweetness drowned,
Is the chord that's touched in kindness
    By the dearest love of life,
And the power to trill that chordlet
    Is but given to a Wife.

Other voices may be gifted
    With a sweet melodeous tone,
But their notes may be forgotten
    And become to us unknown.
While that silver, silken chordlet
    Thrills forever all through life,
When one word, in love tones given,
    Falls upon it from a Wife.

LIFE'S WARP AND WOOF,

Our life is a gorgeous tapestry.
    And we weave it day by day;
        And the threads will run
        And the form be spun
    Let us weave it as we may.

Each coming joy is a golden thread
    And we merrily pass it through;
        And we watch it shine
        As we gladly twine
    The golden glory true.

But a sorrow comes and our aching hearts
    Beat slow as we weave it in;
        And we will not know
        That our earthly woe
    Makes brigther the crowns we win,

But we only see the earthly warp,
　　God from us the woof doth hide,
　　　　And where shadows lie
　　　　To our earthly eye
　　It is light on the other side.

THE HEART'S ANGUISH.

I have wandered long and lonely,
Dreaming of the time when only
Love and gladness filled my heart,
    Filled my heart with brightest joy;
When no thought of woe corroding,
All my life was downward loading
With an undefined foreboding
    Of the cankerous alloy
Which the world at large was filling,
Hopes and joys, forever killing,
As a demon grim distilling
    All the essences of woo,
Poured his murd'rous, vap'rous potions,
Making hellish dark commotions
    In the inmost soul of man,
Till he curses all his being,
    Curses heav'ns mighty plan
    O'er each pain extorted throe.

Oh! those mem'ries ever falling
On my heart still keep recalling

All on earth I had to love,
    All on earth I loved and lost!
And, my anguished heart still throbbing,
Ever throbbing, dully throbbing,
Seems the torture racked sobbing
    Of a soul all tempest tossed;
And my spirit in its groaning,
Still is moaning, ever moaning,
Every hope of joy dethroning,
    Sinking deeper in its woe;
All the awful horror drinking,
All the past and present linking
    In a horrible design,
Gloats in frenzy o'er the picture,
    O'er the picture that is mine,
    And, that only I may know.

Oh! the deep and mighty anguish
Wherein now my soul doth languish!
With no ray of happiness,
    With no hope forevermore;
And, despair now falling round me,
In its endless chain hath bound me,
While the demon still doth wound me

To my heart's deep inmost core.
Oh, the deep abyss appalling,
Into which my soul is falling,
Where the loathsome vipers crawling
　　Deep, and deeper make my woe!
And, my soul in horror starting
From the baleful glances darting
　　Through each lava-flooded vein,
Strives to mount from out the horror,
　　Striving, but to fall again,
　　While the fiends their thriumph show.

Oh, ye fiends in triumph yelling!
On my heart your vict'ry knelling,
In your wild demoniac glee
　　Tearing at my heart-strings sore;
With your fiery glances flashing,
All my soul with torture lashing,
Like a whip of scorpions gashing,
　　Gashing, deeper, more and more;
Oh, ye demons hear my moaning!
Hear my horror haunted groaning!
With a mighty deep detoning
　　Of a mournful, ceaseless woe:

See my hands to you outreaching
In a frantic wild beseeching,
     Hear the pray'rs I madly pour !
Some respite from this mad torture,
     Grant me, grant me I implore !
     To my soul some mercy show!

Oh, ye hellish fiends ungranting !
In your demon glory panting,
I have sued to you for nought,
     Supplicated you in vain;
For, your breasts with rapture swelling,
Feel a glory in thus kneeling
Doom, unto my ear thus telling
     All its agony and pain;
Oh, ye fiends of hell infernal !
With your pow'r almost supernal,
Reaching through all time eternal,
     Here I mock you with my woe !
Here I tear my soul asunder,
Tell to you in tones of thunder
     I defy you !—This I tell,
While the mighty tones resounding

Shout defiance thro' all hell,
Which to you in scorn I throw.

Now, the waves of hell outpouring
O'er my soul are madly roaring,
And they seethe, and roll, and roar,
    With a mighty monotone!
And each word from hence ascending,
From my heart now stricken, bending,
'Neath its load for life unending
    Can be nothing but a groan;
And this awful deep despairing,
And this fiery torture tearing,
At my soul forever wearing
    Its unchanging mantle,—woe
Forces from my heart wild beating,
This one angusihed cry repeating
    Up to heaven, down to hell;
Shall eternity but be
    To my heart a fun'ral knell,
    Shall I never mercy know !

Oh, thou God above, all seeing !
Oh, thou Author of my being !

Hear my supplicating moan,
    Hear my wild despairing cry!
At thy throne in suppliance kneeling,
All my heart to Thee revealing,
Hear my frantic, wild appealing,
    Save me, Maker, or I die!
All my wrongs to Thee now bringing,
And to Thee now only clinging,
While the angels, ever winging,
    Bear aloft my weight of woe.
Up, from out my dark surrounding,
From the darts my heart still wounding,
    Lift me, lift me I implore!
Up from out the hadean darkness,
    Lift my soul forevermore!
    And thy mercy to me show!

What?—my weary burden lightens,
And my darkened spirit brightens,
Hast thou heard me, oh, Jehovah!
    Hast thou heard my soul worn cry?
Yes! I see thy mercy bending,
Like a halo bright descending
From a love that knows no ending.

From its fountain head on high;
And my spirit upward bounding,
Up, from out its dark surrounding,
Song of praise to Thee is sounding
    As it mounts from out its woe.
And my praises up ascending,
Shall from henceforth know no ending,
    But eternally shall sound
One continuous mighty anthem
    For this peace unending found,
    Which now o'er my soul doth flow.

Now, and o'er my senses stealing,
Comes that gentle calm revealing
Of a heaven given peace,
    Of a peace forevermore;
And my soul its sweet rest gaining,
And the heav'n nectar draining,
Sees its mighty anguish waning
    And its praise it doth outpour;
And the heaven ever nearing
Sendeth forth its sunlight cheering,
And my sorrow disappearing
    · Leaves no semblance of the woe

That hath now no power o'er me,
For within the land before me
　　There can enter no alloy,
To be mingled with the glory
　　Of that pure and endless joy,
　　Which my soul shall henceforth know.

' THE END.

www.ingramcontent.com/pod-product-compliance
Lightning Source LLC
Chambersburg PA
CBHW030551270326
41927CB00008B/1602